THE FRUSTRATED ONES

poems by

Kathleen Radigan

Finishing Line Press
Georgetown, Kentucky

THE
FRUSTRATED ONES

Copyright © 2021 by Kathleen Radigan
ISBN 978-1-64662-524-6 First Edition
All rights reserved under International and Pan-American Copyright Conventions.
No part of this book may be reproduced in any manner whatsoever without written permission from the publisher, except in the case of brief quotations embodied in critical articles and reviews.

ACKNOWLEDGMENTS

Thanks to the following journals for first featuring these poems:

A Little Song in *The Adroit Journal*
My Mother in *Vagabond City Lit*
Free Chair in *Dialogist*
Doom Seuss and Echocardiogram in *apt*
Eve, Plea to God, and Augur in the anthology *"If You're Not Happy Now."* Broadstone Books, March 2019. Monarch in *New Ohio Review*
Babysitting in *Carve Magazine*
Twenty-Two in *The Antigonish Review*
Sims 2 and My Grandmother Lived in a Tree in *Storyscape*

Publisher: Leah Huete de Maines
Editor: Christen Kincaid
Cover Art: Kathryn LaMontagne
Author Photo: Kathleen Radigan
Cover Design: Elizabeth Maines McCleavy

Order online: www.finishinglinepress.com
also available on amazon.com

Author inquiries and mail orders:
Finishing Line Press
PO Box 1626
Georgetown, Kentucky 40324
USA

Table of Contents

A Little Song 1
My Mother 2
Twenty-Two 3
Worm in the Violent World 4
Prayer 5
Ode to Zoloft 6
Babysitting 7
Twelve 8
I Forget it All 9
Fission 10
That Evening 11
Dying in Kilkenny 12
I Forgot to Tell You 13
Friend 14
Plea to God 15
Eve 16
Happy 17
Worm Moon 18
Sims 2 19
My Grandmother Lived in a Tree 20
The Frustrated Ones 21
Monarch 22
Free Chair 23
Carnival 24
Girl on a Ferris Wheel 25
First Party 26
Doom Seuss 27
Dispatch from Heaven 28
Echocardiogram 29
Augur 31
For My Organs, After Eating Cheese 32
Hot Meat 33

"There is no satisfaction whatever at any time. There is on a queer, divine dissatisfaction, a blessed unrest that keeps us marching."
—Martha Graham

"A wrong number occurs to you in the middle
Of the night, you dial it, it rings just in time
To save the house."
—Robert Bly, "People Like Us"

A LITTLE SONG

Because crickets' throats dry up like dunes
unless they sing, the rest of us must listen
to white whistling. All summer, petals of paint
snap off the porch steps. The sky slides open.
Pauses slip into the grass.

My sister and I try breathing without sound.
Our hearts, heat thunder. Ears to the sky.
Listening to stars' quiet piles of light.
We sit and chirp for birds on power lines.
We'll probably both be lonely for a long time.

MY MOTHER

Met my father
in summer
at some wedding.

She won't say if they kissed,
or felt clairvoyant twinges
during Vows.

"That's private."

She cracks pistachios,
flings the shells
out the car window.

I bet her hair hung
like a waterfall—
cheeks sunburnt,

green-eyed in the pew.
Kept clean fingernails,
knew her grandmother's friends

by name.
She's like tarot now,
all predictions.

Hides old selves
under starched shirts.
Talks like a bottle rocket.

Radiologists call
from a bright-ceilinged world
where death and life

are zig-zags on a screen.
Can it be true?
Each day is dead so soon.

TWENTY-TWO

At last the dermatologist
returned my call.
Scratch my scalp. It flakes.

First snow. Stung nose,
snot rose, petalled tissues.
Thin shoes, raw toes.

Slimy eyes and tongue.
My beautiful body is rancid.
I want to have babies.

To lie down
with my red-mouthed babies
beneath deadbeat stars

and kick my shoes off far
as I can fling them.
Gutters gargle car oil,

dog shit, auburn vomit.
Since age twelve,
I've grieved

each burnt red pad stain.
My eggs,
those soft lost daughters.

(Will I forget my babies?
Will they bury me?
Did I dream them?)

I will renounce all others
when I meet them. I mean it.
I do not mince words.

WORM IN THE VIOLENT WORLD

I couldn't help it.
I tunneled toward the lust:
        Man, mouse, fungus.
        Eyeless, I cavorted roots,

the underworld's gnarled thruways,
and burrowed toward red filaments of interest—
        my body leaking glue.

        Splintered, I begot
        a twin.
        Hark! Rejuvenation.

Sliced down to spine, I made a living
limb from the numb din of my pain.

        Do I begrudge my sadder half?
        That my wound churned a path
        from herself? No, my sister and I will live
        forever. We are singing underneath you
        in the slime.

PRAYER

My mother won't read
the oncology report.

Walks the dog
by the sea.
Drives for hours
under a bruised sky
and returns
with vanilla ice cream.

On my bed, she lays out
a corduroy skirt for church,
where stained glass
tints us pink.

ODE TO ZOLOFT

I contain so much, I must be contained:
Clouds and towels, spools of rain.
O Sertraline, herb up my brain.
Lick me in halo, seal me in feeling.
I am in my childhood bedroom
kicking the ceiling.

Dear warm oracle, dear jelly cloud:
Your rules are mine now.
I've eaten of your blues five years.
Watch me sleep without weeping.
Watch me grieve without dying.
Aren't you impressed?

Swallow, gem. Follow, calm.
Dissolve me here. I am a red
charm, a confetti flair. This peace is false
and I don't care.

BABYSITTING

In the star-lamp
your skin glows,

lemony. Gelatin
body. You lob

saliva globes,
blink between bars,

chew a bear's ear.
I once sat like you

in a plastic crib,
sheets wet.

I swished my net
through warm dream

cellars, needing.
Never knowing

I'd grow teeth.

TWELVE
    After Marie Howe

We dared ourselves—pattered
down the back-stairs.

Quiet as fish
past your parents' room.

Knife of light in the door.
The screen clicked.

We lunged over your dad's
tomato patch, drenched yard,

whole humid world. Streetlights
in neighbors' pools.

"In Never Land
we'll be little boys forever."

We lay in the plastic play house
and practiced kissing.

Our tongues flicked,
little flashlights in the dark.

Fruit heat of shampoo
and breathing. Earwigs burrowed

in the pink stove, glistening
piles of skins. You said,

"I'm so afraid to have sex someday."
I said, "Me too." We stared

at the plastic walls
of all we knew, moving through.

I FORGET IT ALL

Except the way he held me
in the pool,
his pupils gone
jeweled, watchful.

His chest blissed
in porchlights,
the hum of him
under my hands.

How he said, rheumy
from moonshine,
"If I wasn't with her,
 I'd want to be with you."

I could see, in the minute,
it was true. I was twenty-three.
Inside me were thousands
of wires.

FISSION

I'd seen the news. They'd cranked
the Doomsday clock a notch to twelve.

The world would soon expire
but I could only think of Paul, my crush.

To bite his lip, to slip
into his light, to sing his lids.

I told him in the rainy parking lot.
"Thanks," he hedged.

A tongue fell over the sun.
I never dreamed of him.

When I did, he showed up
as a swell of red

I called into my body like a sleep.
Diplomats from every nation

gathered to diffuse the bomb.
The sadness did not matter.

My atoms clung together.
Shuttered houses shook.

I cried and cried for Paul. For Paul.
The paint dripped down the walls.

THAT EVENING

You stood in my kitchen
eating canned peaches

opening and shutting like an eye
with mollusk mouth twitching

All week I'd thought of you
crushed out   sweats   heart palps

the whole works   washed the pans
flicked the lights   changed the music

shook the rug out   Then you were there

with acid mouth and   violet tongue
your face   a bare bulb

the wine going down

down   willing it

DYING IN KILKENNY
For Susannah

Grow numb in a straw house
as dogs roll in sawdust.

Kiss the billy-goat in the road
your horned girl, willful mule.

Drink gin with ginseng
under the brutal moon.

Dying's a chore.
Hearing another world's

burnt roar. Shake bats
from the umbrella.

Let lambs graze in rain.
Kick the cock, save the chick.

Kneel to vomit. Bake a pie.
Die drunk under the Northern lights.

Time thins here,
smoke off manure.

I FORGOT TO TELL YOU

I bought strawberry jam   It's dappled with seeds
That's the difference between jam and jelly
Did your mother ever tell you?

Do you know of a good piece of toast I can burrow inside?
I like the way bread melds to my stony top palate
I must say   I wish I could will my mouth bigger
and fit a whole hand inside   I'd be fascinating then

Would you be impressed?   Yes, and what else?
I would eat my own leg and spit it back out
I would do it every day   It would become a sort of job

I'd stand beside a bell-tower   clang the bell every hour
swallow an audience volunteer   and spit her out quick
her whole constitution changed

FRIEND

Then it was you and I inside the house.

You asked, "Why should I live?" You and I in the lamp.
Boots and yells outside. The winter parties—
blades of sound, feral and far-away.

I unclipped my earrings and climbed in beside you.
"I don't know why."

You breathed slow, tugged to leaden sleep.
I loved you. Our wrists turned up, we dropped into blue silence.

PLEA TO GOD

Before You knock me up, let me birth fistfuls of gold moths.
Water snakes. Let ants dance out my mouth.
I'm only fourteen. I haven't felt a lot. I want sisters who are lizards.
Peer inside my belly full of animals: a circus, three thousand
evolutionary years.

I'll die a good virgin. I'll lie by him when it rains inside.
I'll lick his wounds, lock my knees, shelter him in spine.

Prophets say he's destined for a salt grave.
I'll water his bones with tears.
But first I want gardens. Moony daughters whose braces collect sun.
A pool of Your saliva as an emblem.

EVE

Forgive me. I've eaten your clementines.
Skin of vines, sinful rot.

I am a rib-made mistress. Seed in my lungs.
Wet rapes. We are your inmates:

the temptress and the ape.
Tore blooms off your fruit tree,

bored of bramble
and the animals' scared scuttle.

Forgive me, heart blinking
through my hunger.

They were cold. With Eden dead,
Adam will eat me soon.

See how he eyes my thighs,
strokes my spine with a knife.

Calls me the new fruit,
drooling to take my life.

HAPPY

The grief I've known
is an almond in my throat.

Mom and I drink wine.
"Some of my friends' parents," I say,

"Don't love each other anymore."
She sucks her teeth.

"All these shotgun weddings.
Say they're in love after six months."

"You can't know," she says,
"Who that person will be."

She says, "Maybe after ten fine years
he'll punch you till your teeth bleed."

"You have no idea," she says,
"What heartbreak is.

You have a new boyfriend,
good grades—if you're not happy now,

when will you ever be?"

WORM MOON

She says, "I think of his mind
like the television screen
when he turns it off at bedtime.

The picture used to reach the edges
but shrinks further to the middle
every year now."

I think of his mind
like the frozen ground
when he picks me up

from the bus station at night.
"Made this drive every day
for fifty years."

I say, "Nice big moon up there."
He says, "Farmers call it
worm moon.

First of spring,
it tells the worms to look up.
Soil's begun to thaw."

He sometimes fishes such facts
out of the frozen lake, the static
in his brain.

"The man who owned
the house before us installed the hoop.
An NBA player and his son."

I can't listen. I am thinking
of worms tilting in the dark
like fetuses

or astronauts,
their heads drawn blind
until they see the stars.

SIMS 2

Grandma Sim glimmered,
creased from laughing.
I sailed her through
the kitchen with a click,
blew rooms onto her house.
I gave her pant-suits,
a quaint ranch
with a pool and porch.
Her slippers swished.
She ribbed her kids
in gibberish. Gestured
with pruning shears.
She watched the news.
Woohooed her blank husband
atop a blue duvet.
I sliced off the roof to see.
Her yard a ghostly paradise of trees.

One day, I left my seat
to make a snack. When I got back,
she was dead. Splayed on the rug,
her pants unstained.
Her daughter screeched.
Her son knelt, muttering.
Then they sat down
in arm chairs,
awaiting instruction.

MY GRANDMOTHER LIVED IN A TREE

No—my grandmother lived in a tenement house.
When she was a girl, two cats on her lawn turned to dust.
When she was a girl, she sensed me coming.

She called my name and her voice shattered.
My grandmother was born in a dance hall.
No—a fountain sour with pennies.

Her mother brought her up in the Depression.
Her mother made a few bucks wrestling men.
Once, she wrestled the moon and won.

Hung his skin on the wall as a prize.
He was dead. No, some moon was still inside.
My grandmother knew. She winked and he grew

doughy with ardor. They had a secret code, those two
so he let her live forever. No—she's dying
in the den now as the TV repeats nature shows.

"The camera men fed steaks
to those hyenas. Call this nature.
What liars. Pulling tricks to fill a time slot."

No—she's sleeping. In the next room,
I am boiling water. Gripped by a grief,
I dial the future on her rotary phone.

I ask, "Are you in there?" A voice yesses inside.
It is my granddaughter waiting to be
in the terrible next world over.

She tells me, "It's coming: the beautiful future.
You who knew what to say
will be made helpless."

THE FRUSTRATED ONES

Two moths got in the apartment. Now dead leaves
heave over my pomegranate candle flame.

Each little Icarus dares the other, draws back.
Hovers. Gathers trust.

When the lamps click off, their never-touched wings
flutter in the cupboard molting dust,

dreaming of sun, rocking all night in their abdomens.

MONARCH

In the garden, I cup a hand
before you. Strain my wrist.
Will you to perch.

A nearby woman grips her cane.
"Young lady. If you touch them,
they die."

Born again from a gauze
coffin, you're black-winged,
fragile on a wax leaf.

In the heat of a weeklong life
you batter between
fluorescents and dahlias, legs thinner

than wires. Float over tendriled
chrysanthemum heads.
Tease everything

— hands, canes, stems, with feathery
suggestion. I want to chew you
to taste each metallic

wing, to look so beautiful
that being touched
just once would kill me.

FREE CHAIR

Orphaned by indifferent kings
on a roadside, I find you glazed with rain.

Your wicker glitters with colorless light,
gnarled urchin the sea coughed out.

My skin calcifies, curls and peels.
I chew sun-poison paint flecks beside you

on the highway. We aging exhibitionists
dim under wind wear. We two vagabonds

hunch in ourselves, listen for a mother
in the car screech.

CARNIVAL

Streetlights in your hair, hands
wheel-bound. Tires squelch the street.
I relish your confessions, gifts
of reveal, your neck's delicious cracks.

We park by seashore clam-shacks
and boardwalk heat seeps in our bones.
Low tide smells like summer thighs,
bleeds green inside the moon's old pull.
We watch dunes stir and miles away,
the rollercoaster clench before a plunge.

I love the world, though it's ugly.
You're a woman and my friend.
Our love beats on our necks in sticky wind:
a clam cakes' pillow insides,
a fistful of soft hair, a tender fist.

GIRL ON A FERRIS WHEEL

Three bucks to sit in a steel box
and lord over the mirror hall,
the claw machines blitzed in bulbs.
I'm alone on the lit skeleton
craving True Love, or a shoulder
bone to lean on till my ear aches.

Down in the leopard light,
a toothless man spits brown
into a plastic bag. Boys duck
under plush ropes to jack
the fortune teller's globe.

I lift both arms over the screeching
crowd and mouths: *I Love You.*
To feel something I haven't.
Fresh paint on an outer ring
of heaven. In suspension,
the ride sends on. It's snowing
a glittery little. Wet slick
on my palms.

FIRST PARTY

Bare shouldered.
Moon under tongue.

Trampoline puddled
in bathing suit runoff.

Deck-chair grandpas
tanked on gin.

Spin-the-bottle
in the road.

Whack of lips
the headlights scatter.

Golf course
sealed in hills.

His yellow breath
and tongue.

Don't worry kid,
the feeling's

coming soon,
soon.

DOOM SEUSS

Oh, today you are vapor! Downstream past the womb—
beyond stars, guns and needles, dried blood, your new tomb.

Congratulations! Today you depart. Was it cancer,
a car crash, a fire in the dark? You had brains in your head!

You had feet in your shoes! You played shortstop, felt pain,
learned the sax, sang the blues!

You were mostly alone, and you knew what you knew
though some nights you dressed up, chugging drinks that were blue,

arm in arm with your friends, stumbling wet avenues!
Now your friends' lives will blur as their eyes blot and blot.

From here on, you are gone. You are only a thought.
They'll reflect on your kindness and shrink all your faults.

They'll forget what you screamed, you will fade into schmaltz.
Is it warm where you are? Do you foam? Are you formless?

Do you miss us already? Bathrobed and gorgeous?
Remember sunrise from the summer camp tent,

and autumn leaves scattered on branches all bent
or the person you loved caught in sleep, and their scent?

Oh, it's sweet to remember the places you went.

DISPATCH FROM HEAVEN

I don't miss bomb drills or dry Easter lamb-chops.
I miss flies with dirt-streaked wings.
Talk radio, pond brine to my knees.
Waitresses with tattooed ankles, diner ketchup bottles,
cities stacked like milk cartons
polluting the universe, pumping it with light.
I miss my brain before I ever grieved.

Steam off coffee, slipping under sleep's foam rim.
Flying dreams, the salt space a lost tooth leaves.
I miss the field trip to the polluted lake, how we unpacked
our logbooks, screamed camp songs. The water black like tea.

ECHOCARDIOGRAM

The heart's a warren of changeable water
                                        a shoddy shadowy whatever

Its technical image is feathers   or the space in a sneeze

between lip and quiver

I got scared my heart was marrowing out its shift
in my ribs' latticed blackness

I know I could be more grassy in general
I could walk in tall woods   and kiss sapling's backs

Pry up their bark's leather briar underneath and touch thumbholes
sweet water trickling   down my eyes

I used to commune with spirits in knotholes

white sap congealed on trees' divots
I was a lonely kid and joy ballooned from me
I talked to deer but they said nothing

I tell you these things   because I want you to know

I'd like to live in primal haze   a half-asleep launch toward the toilet
To hang my bones on an earring stand
and sleep in a jelly-world as organs loll in fat

                        My heart on the screen was a shadow mouth

I was off-put by how it announced itself
                                      Exposed its pretzel shape

I hated its mouth breathing
                    How it wearied of its metronome task
prone in its woodland cabin

I wondered   Was it hungry? Did it want to go for a walk?
Trying to suck up each day's smear of light
                                    So far my heart endures

like Jonah   awash in the limp dark

AUGUR

The storm blows down
a hundred-year-old pine
just inches from the house.

Now, out the kitchen window,
my mother looks over
its hulk trunk, lichen-swollen.

The threat passed over,
left contrails on her breasts.
When they noticed,

doctors sank gloved hands
inside her skin
and pulled out the tumor,

a dove from a hat.
Her slippers all night
through the kitchen.

The countertop shines
in the dark
like a deer's eye.

She pounds chicken
with murderous force.
Parts meat with a knife

and gut-glossed hands.
Pulls heart from carcass, keeps
a wishbone for after.

FOR MY ORGANS, AFTER EATING CHEESE

I'm tired of this milky talk
passed between you all
in solemn rumbles. Gossip of bile
bubbling into darkness
down the charnels.

O water-state, my carelessness
has swollen your red bodies
into loaves. O lonely nation:
eyes pining for privacy,
lungs, blue-twinned
and Sisyphan. O tangle
of loose cables. Meat bouquet.

Forgive me, wet pets.
Shake off your rain-jackets.
Tell me the news. Do you live
to serve me, or do your own
regrets consume?

HOT MEAT

Laid on the balcony at last,
I take a Xanax. Peel down
to underwear. My bones
are sun-rinsed amber, blood is
wine. My shut eyes swim
with colors. I am a blind

cloud. Men tremble below.
My neck is an altar. Convex
of belly, a stained-glass cathedral.

My thighs are skin and tissue.
They are mine.

Down on earth, men bounce
basketballs in rain on coal-soft
sidewalks. Dark suns dribble
and dribble in communion.

For a breath, they all look up at me
and ask their quiet questions.

Additional Acknowledgments

Thank you to my family—Mom, Dad, and Maura.

Thank you to my teachers and mentors—Marion Wrye, Blanche Boyd, Erica Hunt, Amy Bloom, Karl Kirchwey, Gail Mazur, Robert Pinsky, and Cynthia Cruz— for your wisdom and generosity.

Thank you to the following people for reading and responding to these poems in different iterations, and for being truly incredible friends—

Davis Alianiello, Delali Ayivor, Rebecca Brill, Isabel Bartholomew, Duy Doan, Maggie Dunleavy, Madeline Gilmore, Stefania Gomez, Libby Goss, Daniel Hardisty, Rebecca Levi, Sarah Wagner Miller, Lauren Peat, Anna Strzempko, Emily Yaremchuk, and Grace Yun.

Thank you to Kathryn LaMontagne for the cover art, and for knowing exactly what I meant.

Thank you to Wesleyan University English Department for granting me an Olin Fellowship and a Winchester Fellowship.

Thanks also to Wesleyan University English Department for granting me the Sarah Hannah and Sophie Reed prizes for Poetry.

Thank you to Bob Hildreth and Boston University for granting me a Robert Pinsky Travel Fellowship.

Thank you to Jason Koo & co for a Brooklyn Poets Fellowship.

www.ingramcontent.com/pod-product-compliance
Lightning Source LLC
LaVergne TN
LVHW041558070426
835507LV00011B/1153